Because What Else Could I Do

PITT POETRY SERIES

Ed Ochester, Editor

Because What Else Could I Do

for Daniel Stern
with wonderful memories,
and warmest wishes

Martha Collins

Martha Collins

UNIVERSITY OF PITTSBURGH PRESS

Published by the University of Pittsburgh Press, Pittsburgh, Pa., 15260

Manufactured in the United States of America

Printed on acid-free paper

10 9 8 7 6 5 4 3 2 1

ISBN 13: 978-0-8229-6591-6

ISBN 10: 0-8229-6591-7

Cover art: Doris Salcedo, *Disremembered I*,

2014. Sewing needles and silk thread,

35 × 21½ × 6¼ in. (89 × 55 × 16 cm).

Cover design: Joel W. Coggins

Ted

April 3, 1938–September 2, 2016

*they're coming to get
me arrest jail horrible
problem something*

*stupid decades
ago a legal mistake I
won't be coming back*

*to the house that key
is on the shelf in the*

please try to forgive

almost thirty years you in your

house I in mine every week

end here or there there was

no question only whether here

or there there was no question

that September morning you drove
into your driveway at 7:30 just

as I was fetching the papers, drove
from the wrong direction, I thought

and later that day would think
you might have been seeking a place—

but you really went to the gym
that morning, at 6:19, the woman

said, *Such a gentle man*, everyone
said, you went to the gym

each day, taking care of yourself,
1,243 times, the woman told me

can walk you there, glasses

folded and left in your car

your blue striped shirt, shorts, your

can walk you there or almost

there but cannot

cannot cannot please

don't go please

where did you drive
        how far, how long

did you drive past your house
        where I wasn't then was

did music play that long afternoon
        the Handel you loved

how long did you sit in your car before
        the shift to park, the key

you and you and you and you and

you still warm your face your neck your

hand still warm your you but not

your you you went you left

behind your you not you so cold

you not you

these oranges you bought
these coins you touched

the notes you wrote
this pen you used

the car you drove
that long afternoon

the belt you wore
the ring they removed

the key you hid
the door you closed

you read the papers or turned
the pages so quickly I was still
on the front page you tore

out the weather as always and
must have showered and changed
while I went to the gym and

must have written the tiny
notes and signed the statement
you wrote for your colleagues and

while I was in the shower called
the people who'd called the week
before and called again that morning

at *10:23* the machine said *final notice*
IRS and got in your car and drove

*officially a final
notice from IRS
to inform you IRS*

*is filing a lawsuit
against you to get
more information*

*call our department
number   I repeat*

the week before   the first

call   *IRS* said   *arrest*   you talked

for two hours   *arrest*   you told

me you called   them back   I went

to the IRS site   *we never call*

threaten arrest   it said   *scam*

and you   said   I thought   okay

Three days after I thought you'd agreed *scammers*
you said *It's the IRS pretending they're scammers*

you said *Or it's scammers who know I'm being arrested*
you said *I have to stay home   to be arrested*

Speechless, stunned I finally said *I'm coming
down there, not because I believe they're coming*

but Love because   because— but you'd already gone
their way, your good mind arrested, already gone

thought they wouldn't call
again, and if they didn't

call or come then yes you'd get
some help you said, thought every

day they didn't call or come
was bringing you back to

yourself oh Love I thought—

arrest   you they   said they

got your attention

by force   of

I couldn't   stop you from

stopping   yourself

you thought from

being   arrested from

stopping   yourself

from being

your last meal, cereal
measured, yogurt, juice,
muffin, a little marmalade

and coffee, a little left,
as you always left
it, in your cup

and why not the river the
beautiful the only a mile
away you could have

might have

didn't want

days before when you   told me your colleague

who did what he did   (in case I remembered)

had other reasons not   just a legal mistake—

I thought you meant   you wouldn't because

there was just the legal   mistake you imagined

you'd made but maybe   you meant you had

other maybe   health or maybe   even before

the calls if you   had other   I'll never know

back I go back and do it over it's
7:30 I drop the papers and put
my arms around you and tell you—

back I go back it's the week before
I put my arms around you and say

I will never let you go if those
people come to take you away I
will not let you go I say I—

what did I

what if I'd

what could I

what should I

if I had

could have

black car on the street
could be your car, could be

you if they hadn't called
that second time, or the first—

if you hadn't seen (did you see?)
the police car parked in front

of your house, the police I called
because you hadn't come back

for lunch— or perhaps if I hadn't
said, two weeks before, but that

was about how we could have lived
in your house if you or I . . . how

we could have driven to mine oh
Love if only only you could be

I alone in a restaurant
and what is left of you at home

in a plastic box on your dresser where
you kept your socks and put your change—

and what will I do at home in my own
house, what will I do with my one

spoon and my wide bed, what
will I do without without

September on
your calendar here your
calendar there you turned

the pages you wrote
a check on September
first but you cancelled

October the doctor
roof reunion *Need
to cancel* you wrote

then *Done*

22

US indicts
dozens who posed

as IRS agents
threatened arrest

150,000 victims
$300 million

thought of writing for all
the world *those bastards they* but

how could I so *gentle* you I would
not say write any thing I'd written

you into my other my love though
not the sonnets I'd meant to write

—but what did you think I would do?

probably didn't cross your mind I
didn't cross your mind you were

but now what else can I do?

In the dream we are standing
together in your kitchen we have just

finished the dishes you are wearing
your blue shirt with the white

stripes I have my arm across
your shoulders and I am saying *I*

am so glad (and then my hand)
so glad we could save you

November 8, 2016

the what you will never
the what you missed

the reddening map
the can't be true

the what the climate
the send them back

the end the public
the health the rights

the black the planet
the white the white

the how did we fail
the what can we do

the how did I fail
the nothing to do

I have to tell you I'm   sleeping with

a snowy owl   a kids'   puppet my friend

sent me   it has   a stick so you can turn

the head all the way   around   the way

owls do   but I can't feel   the stick her

wings   wrap part way   around   me

and comfort   me I   know she is a   she

because she has   black spots   and I

should also mention   the photograph

taken by   another friend   who gave it

to me it's   sitting   on my desk beside

some pictures   of you it's   a snowy

owl and she   is flying   toward you

snow is over

everything is covered

with you white

over the lines

of the trees reverse

writing silent

drove your car   home

from your   car you drove

first time I   since you drove

last time you   freezing rain

grief's a lot   like fear someone

wrote I did   not feel safe and

now none   of us feels safe is

this the end   of every our

end of our   sun that day

fear was your   come to take

you put   you away   fear's

a lot   like grief   if we

could stop   beside the road

and hold   your fear my

over   pass   over

the no   don't go

past the   please

don't go   over the   over

and over   again the over-

pass   please no

What do you care, you'll be dead
you said, years ago, and your

daughter stopped (we were walking)
and said, *But Dad, that's her legacy.*

You didn't understand, you must
have thought the world would die

with you, you must have counted
on her, your son, their kids,

or maybe you didn't count at all,
you thought you could leave it all

behind, not just your things but all
the rest, you thought it would not

thought you could let it thought
you could make it all go away

in the back of a drawer

in an unmarked folder

a book about how to when

your last commute: I drove
you in your car played
Handel all the way

walked you up my stairs
this last weekend we
will be together

~

ashes on my dresser
now I tried to put
them beside my bed

but what could I do
with a plastic box
in a thick paper bag

~

so I put the armadillo
I bought you on top
of the box with the little

gray goose I bought
you because you loved
the song *the old gray goose is*

I want you   to know I'm glad

you don't know but   I want you

to have   been right   that maybe

it will not be   so bad I want

you to help me   believe that maybe

it won't be the end   of everything

so from now   on I am going

to keep   you posted   which means

I will have   to read   the papers

not just   the headlines   so I

can keep you   informed   the way

you liked   to be   informed but

of course I'm still   glad you

don't know   don't have   to know

Hello over there with
the armadillo and little
gray goose you'd always

say *Hello there* or just
Hello when we met
on weekends and some

times after we'd settled
into the bed and some
times just after we'd

Love this is almost
our last night together the
night before the night

before Christmas and all
through the house not a
creature is stirring but me

this page

the one I tore out

of the notebook is

just between you

and me

oh   oh   I just saw
you over the edge and—

but no, I'm bringing
you up in your blue

striped shirt, your black
jacket in which you carried

your wallet, some loose
change, the tiny notes

you'd written in that
less than an hour after

the call: one for whoever
found you, and one for me

not so much jump

    as fall into or

        onto a lower

place through loss

    or lack

        of support or

not so much fall as let

    fall as a thing

        once held

in a hand or fall

    as in voice or

        eyes

all fallen away

have entered into
grief as into

a room there are
no windows there is

only this door which I
have closed behind me

the winding road
the bare trees

through bare trees
the gray pond

beside the pond
the bench where you sat

the empty bench
the still pond

across the pond
the two white chairs

the chairs reflected
where I would swim

and when I'd swum
almost back in

you'd get in the water
and meet me there

40

paper bag with   empty box with

almost empty   plastic bag   and on

my hands and on   my jeans   you

some part or   parts   of you from

when we sent   you into   the sea

low   tide so you   easily rode

the lightest   currents   in tiny

explosions   of white   and when

we finished   a sudden   late sun

on the water   of which   you were

becoming   a part   on runnels

between   patches of sand   as if you

were signing   yourself   in silver

In the dream we've disagreed: you've ordered twice
as much fish as we need and when I've complained

you've walked out of the store and left the fish and I've
walked out behind you and into the night in the little

beige heels I wore in the picture I sent before
we met and you've gone to the car but I haven't

followed I'm walking home and home is miles
away in this town which isn't your town or mine

and now it is dark and there are no cars no lights
and I am very afraid: I think I should not be walking

alone and not in these shoes but I am alone and home
is twice as far from here as I ever thought it would be

another beach, the last one we walked

together, hand in hand in the August sun,

and I walked on while you rested there, and now

it is winter and I am here with almost the last

of you in my hand, a tiny part of some parts

of you—your hand, your blue eye, shoulder,

mouth—and I try to gentle you in

to the sea, but a sudden wave rushes over

my feet and the wind catches this part

of some parts of you, and instead you are in

the air and more than before you are on

me: you have met me again, you will not let

me let you go, you are in the sea where you wanted

to be, but you are also in air and sand and earth

where your grandson will bury another small part—

and now I lick my finger and you are in me

as if I had swallowed the fact at last

as if the fact were a mass of lead

as if the mass made a space around it

as if the mass were a tiny planet

as if the planet were you, your life

the one you didn't want anymore

as if what I am were in orbit around you

not as a moon, but as random debris

myself in pieces, space between fact and me

and with you went my summer sun, a friend
or two, and who was there, and with you went

the weeks to come, the months so far (so far,
my one!), my body too, the one I knew

as one of two, though you forgot to take
desire, which now is wrapped in grief's long arms,

and with you went the one I was, that was
—within, without, with you—mostly brave

and largely true, the one I find some moments
in some darkened place of joy, then lose

It's gone, your black car, whose trunk
would open itself for my suitcase, whose seats
would warm us, who came (you came) to me
on weekends for thirteen years and went
to the Cape each summer, went for 163,000
miles, went to the store, the office, the gym—

to the gym that morning, before the second call,
and home to the call, and an hour later went out
and went through half a tank of gas, how
many miles is that, and then—and maybe
this is why I left the tank half full—
you parked and turned the key for the last time

sadder without   the wailing

only this silence   this still

waking   and having

to learn what sleep   forgot

this without   this   this not

report today *official* it said, four
months later, four months after

I'd called and written and called
it finally came and it said not only

your poor head *trauma* chest
trauma lungs broken bones but your

heart was already *severe* already
diseased your poor heart that weighed

380 grams your severe heart heavy
with fear panic shame was blocked oh

Love, my sweet heart, your dear heart
was already hurt and no one knew

I had waited for the report and when at last

the report came I asked and she said since your heart

your brain could also but also said I should ask

another and so I asked and he said organic

and I said are you sure? and he said such sudden

change is always oh Love he was sure so

suddenly muddled your brain your wounded brain

white dream house   filled with gray
paintings of twisted   menacing shapes

and then you're there   and you are saying
we don't have to take   these with us when

we leave for the new   place when we leave
together we can leave   these things behind

so Love it was not the calls, the police car parked
in front of your house, not the legal mistake
you imagined you might have made—

it was not the book you hid, the house where you thought
they would be coming that made you drive
all afternoon, and then park—

it was none of this, I'm told, it was your brain,
hurt, like your heart, a thing that changed you so
you no longer were yourself, your   self—

and so I got   you back

as you were   a friend

says I haven't   been loving

to her but   I have been busy

loving   you   grief's

a form   of love   I read I

cannot tell   my friend but

you as you were   are in

me to   have   and to

in your rust-colored jacket
your blue striped shirt

on your skis, in the woods
on the beach, in the surf

your house, your house
in winter, in spring

in your office chair
in the yard with your kids

in California
in Florence, in Rome

your lilacs before
they broke in the storm

your face, your face
all over now

I want to make you

a mourning shirt a beautiful

thing like the artist made

for the murdered young men

but this would be for me

for us with traces of lost thread

by thread not to manage grief but

needle by needle inserted raw in

the center of our lives to appear

and disappear the absent almost

within   but not   to touch

one month lived that morning over
and over that awful afternoon and

two months wept and wailed I'm sorry
sorry why screamed why in my car and

three months then that news that face
in our faces how but always you and

four months what could I wrote my heart
out wrote your ashes into the sea and

five months finally swallowed the fact and
then the new fact *organic* your brain and

six months wrapped myself in knowing and
now it has been six months to the day since

you drove into your driveway Good morning
my Love   what a mourning   the stars

On the evening of the six-month day I drove

into the hills a rivered town a little café to read

my poems to strangers and friends and at

the end I read *go with me   into that night where one*

will go before   read *moon by night*   read *night-*

night my love   by and by   and there

was silence because (they told me after) when I

read *go* the door opened but no one was there

and when I read   *by*   the door closed

NOTES

I addressed these poems to my husband in the months
following his unexpected death. I wrote them for him, for
his abiding presence. And of course I wrote them for myself.
At the time, I had no intention of publishing them.
But here they are.

22 is extracted from the *New York Times*, October 6, 2016.

53 is based on Doris Salcedo's "Disremembered" sculptures,
several of which appeared in a 2017 exhibit at the Harvard
Art Museums titled *The Materiality of Mourning*. The
poem incorporates some fragments of the artist's
statement about the work.

Parts of this book appeared in *Battery Journal,*
Copper Nickel, and *Plume Poetry*.
My thanks to the editors.